What Do You Think?

Should We Eat Animals?

Andrew Langley

Heinemann Library
Chicago, Illinois

Customer Service 888-454-2279
Visit our website at www.heinemannraintree.com

Editorial: Andrew Farrow and Rebecca Vickers
Design: Steve Mead and Q2A Solutions
Picture Research: Melissa Allison
Production: Alison Parsons

Originated by Chroma Graphics Pte. Ltd.
Printed and bound in China by Leo Paper Group

12 11 10 09 08
10 9 8 7 6 5 4 3 2 1

ISBN: 978-1-4329-0360-2 (hardback)

Library of Congress Cataloging-in-Publication Data
Langley, Andrew.
   Should we eat animals? / Andrew Langley.
      p. cm. -- (What do you think?)
   Includes bibliographical references and index.
   ISBN-13: 978-1-4329-0360-2 (hardback : alk. paper) 1.
Vegetarianism--Juvenile literature.   I. Title.
   TX392.L24 2007
   613.2'62--dc22

                                        2007015728

Acknowledgments
The author and publishers are grateful to the following for permission to reproduce copyright material:

©Alamy Images pp. 23 (Chloe Johnson), 19 (David Hoffman Photo Library), 7 (Dynamic Graphics Group/IT Stock Free), 27 (INSADCO Photography); ©Corbis pp. 4 (Royalty Free), 8, 11 (Archivo Iconografico, S.A.), 36 (Bill Stormont), 15 (Ecoscene/Anthony Cooper), 46 (Peter Johnson), 24 (Phil Schermeister), 47 (zefa/José Fuste Raga); ©FLPA p. 45 (Mary Cherry); ©Getty Images pp. 35, (Allsport/Bob Martin), 51 (Mario Villafuerte), 6 (Stephen Shugerman), 16 (Taxi/Vcl), ©istockphoto.com pp. 29, 41 (Alan Tobey), 13 (Brandon Alms), 49 (George Clerk); ©Nature Picture Library p. 21(Steimer/ARCO); ©OSF pp. 30 (Creatas), 33 (Image Source Limited), 42 (Index Stock Imagery/Katie Deits); ©Punchstock p. 48 (Stockbyte); ©RSPCA Photolibrary p. 18 (E A Janes); ©Still Pictures pp. 39 (Olivier Langrand), 40 (Ron Giling).

Cover photograph of chickens feeding in a large barn, reproduced with permission of Photolibrary (Chris Sharp). Plate is by ©istockphoto.com/Jon Helgason.

The publishers would like to thank Padideh Sabeti for her comments in the preparation of this title.

Every effort has been made to contact copyright holders of any material reproduced in this book. Any omissions will be rectified in subsequent printings if notice is given to the publisher.

Table of Contents

Some words are shown in bold, **like this**. You can find out what they mean by looking in the glossary.

> *Love the taste!*
Many people throughout the world enjoy
eating meat.

Should We Eat Animals?

Most people eat meat. This means that they eat the flesh of animals. Every year, farmers throughout the world raise billions of cows, sheep, pigs, chickens, and other animals. These animals are killed and turned into food for us to eat.

Are you a meat-eater? If so, have you ever stopped to think about the issues involved? You are probably used to having meat as part of your everyday meals. Have you ever wondered whether it is right or wrong to kill animals for food?

There are also many other people who eat no meat at all. These people are called vegetarians. In the United States, about 2 out of every 100 people are vegetarians. In India, the figure is much higher—about 30 people out of every 100 are vegetarians.

Are you a vegetarian? If so, do you think it is wrong to kill animals for food? You have probably taken a firm decision not to eat meat. But how much do you really know about the subject?

People have been arguing about the rights and wrongs of eating animals for hundreds of years. They will continue arguing for a long time to come. Everybody has to eat, so the debate affects us all. We should have the tools and skills to take part in it. This book will help you to join in that debate.

How do you know what to think?

This series of books is called *What Do You Think?* There are two important words in this question—"you" and "think." First, the person involved is *you*, and what matters is your answer to the question. Second, you are being asked to *think*. This does not just mean copying what someone else says, but figuring out your own opinion on a subject.

Suppose somebody asks you, "What is two plus two?" This is a simple question, with just one correct answer: four. If you said "three" or "five," you would be wrong. It is a matter of fact, not opinion.

The title of this book asks a different type of question: "Should we eat animals?" This does not have one correct answer. You cannot state definitely and finally that eating animals is a good or a bad thing. However, you can have an opinion about it.

You need a lot more than strong feelings if you want to form a worthwhile opinion. You should train yourself to think in a balanced way, so that you can look at all sides of a question. You should also be able to give good reasons for what you believe.

What is an argument?

Once you have formed an opinion, the next step is to express it clearly to other people. You can do this by expressing your ideas as an argument. An argument has three parts:

1. Assertion: Stating your opinion simply and briefly
2. Reasoning: Backing up your assertion with good reasons
3. Evidence: Backing up your reasoning with facts and examples.

> *Celebrity campaigners*
>
> **Many famous vegetarians, such as Alicia Silverstone, are actively involved in the animal welfare movement.**

> *What do you think?*
You should be able to back up your opinions
with evidence and good reasoning.

 # How to make your mind up

✔ Look at the evidence
Evidence gives you a firm base on which to build your thinking. But where
will you find it? Look out for news stories in the media. Books and the
Internet will contain more facts and figures. Don't forget that your own
experiences could also be valuable.

✔ Listen to both sides
Don't start out with a set opinion in your head and then try to justify it.
Keep an open mind and listen carefully to the views on both sides, even if
you strongly disagree with them. Remember that this kind of question has
no definite answer. An argument is not won by the person who is right, but
rather by the person who is best at arguing and who has the best evidence
to support his or her view.

✔ Think critically
The most important step of all is to think critically. Learn to ask your
own questions about the evidence you find. Is it fact, or is it just
somebody's idea? Is it honest, or is it **biased** to one side or the other?
Who produced the evidence? Does that person have an interest in trying to
change your views?

> *Ancient hunters*

This prehistoric painting from Cavalls cave in
Spain shows action from a deer hunt.

Why Do We Eat Other Animals?

The very first humans ate plants. They wandered over the landscape gathering leaves, nuts, and other vegetable foods they came across. Then, about 2.5 million years ago, there came a big change. Humans started to eat meat. At first, they probably picked on the remains of bodies killed by hunting animals, such as early tigers and wolves. Later, they learned to hunt for themselves.

What caused this change in eating habits? Nobody knows for certain. Perhaps there was a shortage of tasty plants, and eating animals was the only way to survive. Perhaps people discovered that meat gave them more energy and **protein** than vegetables.

Whatever the reason, meat has been a major part of our diet ever since. In **primitive** societies, hunting for animal food became an important skill. People prayed to their gods for success in hunting, and so meat was strongly linked with religion. The first farmers found that keeping animals in pens and fields was much easier than trying to catch them in the wild.

Today, meat-eating has grown into a huge industry. More than 50 billion animals are killed every year, just to feed humans. Huge numbers of farms, factories, stores, restaurants, and other businesses depend on people's taste for eating meat. The question is: Why do we continue to eat meat?

Are humans made to eat meat?

Many animals, such as lions, eat meat. These hunters are called carnivores (meat-eaters). A far greater number of animals do not eat meat. They live on plant food, such as grass. These vegetarian animals are called herbivores (plant-eaters). There are also a huge number of animals, such as bears, that eat both meat and plants. These are called omnivores.

So, what are humans—carnivores, herbivores, or omnivores? We eat both meat and vegetables. But what are we meant to eat?

How Meat Changed Our Bodies

Meat-eating has impacted the evolution of the human body, scientists reported today at the American Association for the Advancement of Science's annual meeting in Washington, D.C.

Our fondness for a juicy steak triggered a number of adaptations over countless generations. For instance, our jaws have gotten smaller, and we have an improved ability to process **cholesterol** and fat.

Our taste for meat has also led us into some trouble—our teeth are too big for our downsized jaws and most of us need dental work.

When humans switched to meat-eating, they triggered a genetic change that enabled better processing of fats.

"We have an obsession today with fat and cholesterol because we can go to the market and stuff ourselves with it," a scientist said. "But as a species we are relatively immune to the harmful effects of fat and cholesterol. Compared to the great apes, we can handle a diet that's high in fat and cholesterol, and the great apes cannot.

"Even though we have all these problems in terms of heart disease as we get older, if you give a gorilla a diet that a meat-loving man might eat in Western society, that gorilla will die when it's in its twenties; a normal life span might be 50. They just can't handle that kind of diet."

[Source: Hillary Mayell, *National Geographic News*, February 18, 2005]

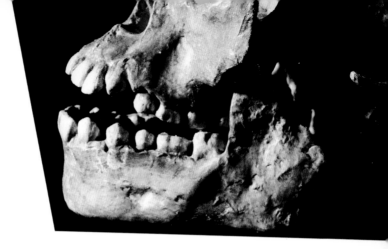

> *Dental development*

A 2-million-year-old human skull shows how teeth evolved to aid meat-eating.

Look carefully at this article to see what evidence you can find to help you form an opinion. For a start, who is giving the evidence? Do you trust the writer to have a balanced and well-informed view?

The article mentions two ways in which the human body has changed since we started to eat animals. These changes made it easier for us to chew and digest meat. But do they mean that we should continue to eat animals?

 Plant-eaters and meat-eaters

Humans belong to a group of animals called mammals. There are over 5,000 different species (types) of mammals.

Herbivorous mammals

Number of species: 5,240 (including elephants, cows, and kangaroos)

Special characteristics:

✔ Big, flat back teeth, good for grinding and chewing tough plants

✔ Complicated stomachs, because plants (for example, grass) take a long time to digest

Carnivorous mammals

Number of species: 270 (including lions and walruses. Many so-called carnivores are actually omnivores—they eat both meat and plants. Foxes, rats, and humans are all omnivores.)

Special characteristics:

✔ Pointed front teeth, good for gripping prey

✔ Sharp back teeth, good for cutting and grinding meat

✔ Simple stomachs, because meat takes a shorter time to digest

Eat meat or starve

Early humans probably started eating meat by accident. But why did they continue to eat it? Why did it become such an important part of our diet? Clearly, it was because meat had some advantages over vegetables for primitive people.

Imagine that you are living 100,000 years ago. You have to spend a lot of time searching for food. If you do not find enough food, you will starve to death.

You do not just need food to fill your stomach. You need good food, with enough proteins, fats, and **vitamins** to keep you strong and healthy.

Wild plants can give you these important substances, but you have to eat a huge amount of them to get enough. This means you have to spend a lot of time searching and gathering the right plants. In winter, or in less fertile parts of the world, this may be an impossible task.

Meat is different. Here, the **nutrients** are packed into a small space. Meat is an excellent source of vitamins, proteins, and fats—and it comes in a handy size. One dead animal can contain enough food for a whole family group. How does this affect your opinion about eating animals?

Did meat give us advantages?

There is no doubt that eating meat caused humans to become the way they are today. We have already seen that our teeth and digestive systems changed to cope with digesting meat. Our jaws became smaller. Our bodies developed in a different way from plant-eating animals.

Meat-eating also led to a much more important change. Our brains grew bigger.

Here is some more evidence:

"[Evidence shows that] human ancestors who roamed the savannas of Africa about 2 million years ago began to include meat in their diets. It was this new meat diet, full of densely packed nutrients, that provided the **catalyst** for human evolution, particularly the growth of the brain."

[Source: Katharine Milton, Department of Physical Anthropology, University of California, Berkeley]

> *Lethal weapon*

This is an ancient stone arrowhead, chipped to a razor-sharp edge. It would have been used in hunting.

The rising of the buffalo men

I rise, I rise,
I, whose tread makes the earth to rumble.
I rise, I rise,
I, in whose thighs there is strength.
I rise, I rise,
I, who whips his back with his tail when in rage.
I rise, I rise,
I, in whose humped shoulder there is power.
I rise, I rise,
I, who shakes his mane when angered.
I rise, I rise,
I, whose horns are sharp and curved.

This is a poem from the Osage, a Native American people. About 200 years ago, they hunted buffalo, which were an important source of food and other materials. They depended on killing these animals to stay alive. What does the poem tell you about the way the hunter feels about the buffalo?

Are humans good at hunting?

Throughout history, some humans have become very skilled hunters. They have figured out how to make cunning traps for catching animals and weapons for killing them. They have learned how to throw spears and to shoot arrows and bullets with great accuracy.

But humans are not great hunters compared to some other animals. Just think about the human body. Is it suited to hunting and catching other creatures? Most of the other carnivores in the animal kingdom are much quicker or stronger or more agile than we are. Moreover, they have claws and long, sharp **canine teeth** for gripping and tearing the skin of their prey. Humans have no claws and only short canine teeth.

Why do we still eat animals?

Today, very few people in the world have to hunt animals to stay alive. Most of us can buy meat (along with a huge variety of other foods) in stores and supermarkets any time we want. Nearly all of our meat comes from animals that have been raised on farms and then killed and prepared in specially equipped **slaughterhouses**.

Why do we continue to eat meat? One obvious reason is that many of us like the taste. The flavor and smell of meat can be very appealing. Meat can be cooked and prepared in thousands of different ways, which make it even tastier. Meat dishes are a central part of most people's diets, just as they have been for hundreds of years.

What is the alternative?

Obviously, humans are free to choose what they wish to eat and what to avoid. Throughout history, some have decided not to eat the flesh of animals. Probably the first vegetarians lived in Egypt about 5,000 years ago. A large proportion of people in the Indian subcontinent have been vegetarian for at least 3,000 years.

In Europe 2,500 years ago, the Greek philosopher Pythagoras and his followers refused to eat meat. He said, "Alas, what wickedness to swallow flesh into our own flesh! For as long as men massacre animals, they will kill each other!"

In more recent centuries, the number of vegetarians in the world has grown steadily. The International Vegetarian Union was formed in 1908.

> *Milking machines*
We consume a huge amount of milk and dairy products every day. Hi-tech milking parlors, like this one, make the milking process quick and hygienic.

 ## What do vegetarians eat?

Lacto-vegetarians do not eat meat or eggs. They can eat any other kind of food, including milk, cheese, butter, and other dairy products.

Ovo-vegetarians do not eat meat or dairy products. They can eat any other kind of food, including eggs, that they do not consider to be meat.

Lacto-ovo-vegetarians do not eat meat. They do eat eggs and dairy products.

Fruitarians only eat raw fruits, nuts, and seeds.

Vegans do not eat any animal products, including meat, fish, eggs, and milk. Some vegans even refuse to eat honey.

> *A broody hen*

A mother hen keeps her eggs warm so the chicks will grow and hatch.

Is It Right To Eat Animals?

How do you decide what is right or wrong? In many cases, it is easy to make up your mind. Almost everyone would agree that stealing is wrong, and that hurting or killing other humans is even more wrong. But is it right or wrong to kill animals and eat them? This decision is much more difficult to make.

There are, of course, two sides to the argument. Are the two sides evenly matched? As you look for evidence, you could easily think that they are not. There seems to be a mountain of evidence and opinion from the vegetarian side, but very little from the meat-eaters. Why is this?

The majority of people throughout the world eat animals. But how many of them spend time thinking about whether it is right or wrong? The probable answer is that very few of them do. Eating meat is just a habit for a huge number of people, and these people do not have a strong opinion on the subject.

In what way are vegetarians different? Many vegetarians have been brought up in societies where it is normal to use animals as food. They have thought about meat-eating and have judged that it is wrong. So, they decide that they will not eat any meat. It is a conscious decision that they are likely to feel passionately about.

The vegetarian viewpoint

Here is what some famous people have had to say about eating animals. Most of them are vegetarians, and they all have strong feelings about meat-eating.

"Truly man is the king of beasts, for his brutality exceeds theirs. We live by the death of others: we are burial places! I have from an early age abjured [rejected] the use of meat, and the time will come when men such as I will look on the murder of animals as they now look on the murder of men."
Leonardo da Vinci, artist (1452–1519)

"There is no **fundamental** difference between man and the higher animals in their mental faculties. The lower animals, like man, manifestly feel pleasure and pain, happiness, and misery."
Charles Darwin, naturalist and scientist (1809–82)

"I have no doubt that it is a part of the destiny of the human race, in its gradual improvement, to leave off eating animals, as surely as the savage tribes have left off eating each other."
Henry David Thoreau, writer (1817–62)

"People may talk as much as they like about their religion, but if it does not teach them to be good and kind to other animals as well as humans, it is all a sham."
Anna Sewell, writer (1820–78)

"Nothing will benefit human health, and increase the chances for survival of life on Earth, as much as the evolution to a Vegetarian Diet."
Albert Einstein, scientist (1879–1955)

"I know, in my soul, that to eat a creature who is raised to be eaten, and who never has a chance to be a real being, is unhealthy. It's like you're just eating misery. You're eating a bitter life."
Alice Walker, writer (born 1944)

> **Animal emotions**
> Do cattle, like this mother and calf, have thoughts and feelings?

> *Animal in distress?*

This sheep is on its way to a market by truck.

First, examine where these quotations came from. Do you know anything about the people who are quoted? If so, do you respect their views? Are you likely to take notice of what they say?

Next, look for evidence. Are there any facts in these quotations? Or are they simply opinions?

Finally, how did these quotations affect you? How did you feel when you read them?

 Types of evidence

Your ideas will always be stronger if you back them up with evidence. This comes in many forms:

1. An example is something that illustrates a point. You may find an example in history or in modern living.

2. Statistics include everything from the total population of a country to the percentage of vegetarians in a city. You will find statistics in all sorts of places—government reports, poll results, and encyclopedias.

3. You can use quotations from experts to support your argument. For example, use a quotation from an expert nutritionist if you are talking about the health aspects of eating meat.

Do animals suffer?

Why do you think people have such strong opinions about eating animals? Many vegetarians believe that animals have feelings and can suffer pain and distress—just like we do. For this reason, animals have just as much right to a happy life as humans have. It is morally wrong to kill them and eat them.

But is this true? Animals have senses, but do they experience pain in the same way we do? Your own experiences will tell you the answer. Perhaps you have seen distressed cats or dogs, with staring eyes, flattened ears, and hunched bodies. It is easy to tell that they are scared. On top of this, scientists have shown that mammals, birds, and even fish definitely feel pain when they are hurt.

Can animals be happy or sad?

Whether animals can be happy or sad is a much more difficult question. Have you ever seen a lamb jumping around in springtime or kittens playing in the sun? They all look pleased about having fun and being alive. But is that just a human's view? We do not really know how the animals themselves feel.

Even so, humans have the power to control animals and their feelings. If we kill an animal, we may be causing harm in several ways. The animal itself may feel pain and fear. We are also taking away its life and the chance of happiness in the future. The death may cause distress to other animals in the group, especially if they are relatives. Do you think we have the right to do these things?

Another way of looking at it

It is easy enough to argue that we should not kill animals. But look at the facts. Humans (including vegetarians) are killing huge numbers of animals every day, for a huge variety of reasons. Most of these deaths are not deliberate. For instance, how many insects get crushed on a car windshield? How many snails and bugs have you stepped on by accident?

We kill plenty of animals because they are pests. Flies, mosquitoes, and other insects can carry diseases that harm us. Rats and mice also spread disease and can cause damage and sometimes injury. So, we use poisons and traps to kill them, often in horrible, painful ways.

> *In the pink*

A young pig enjoys basking in the warmth of the sun.

✔ Who has the biggest brain?

Animal	Brain weight
sperm whale	275 oz. (7,800 g)
elephant	168.6 oz. (4,780 g)
dolphin	56.4 oz. (1,600 g)
human	49.4 oz. (1,400 g)
horse	18.7 oz. (530 g)
cow	15.9 oz. (450 g)
pig	6.35 oz. (180 g)
dog	2.47 oz. (70 g)
chicken	0.04 oz. (1 g)
goldfish	0.003 oz. (0.09 g)

So, the whale has the biggest brain. Does this mean it is the most intelligent animal? Scientists believe that it is not just brain size that counts when measuring intelligence. More important is the **ratio** (proportion) of brain size to body size. Whales and elephants may have huge brains, but they also have huge bodies. The two animals with the best ratio of brain to body size are humans and dolphins.

Religion and eating animals

Where did you learn about the difference between right and wrong? Many people take their ideas about morality from their religion. Many of the world's religions tell us to believe in a universe and a way of living that was created by an all-powerful god or family of gods. So, what does religion have to say about eating animals?

There are many religions, of course, and each of them is different. Moreover, there are groups within every religion that disagree with some of its main teachings. Some forbid their followers from eating any meat, some reject certain kinds of meat, and some allow any kind of diet. Even so, most of the vegetarians in the world do not eat meat for religious reasons.

Do you follow one of these faiths? If so, do you always stick to the rules on eating?

Here is a short survey of the major world religions and their various rules about eating animals. Nearly all of them permit their followers to eat at least some meat. How will this evidence change your opinion? How much of it refers to fact and how much to ancient beliefs?

Hinduism

Hindus believe that all animals have souls. They also believe that we all live many lives, and one of these lives could be lived as an animal. That is a good reason for not killing and eating animals. Hinduism encourages its followers to avoid eating meat because they believe it makes people more aggressive. Vegetables, on the other hand, make us calmer and healthier. All the same, eating meat (apart from beef) is not forbidden.

Jainism

Jainites are strictly vegetarian. Their religion condemns all cruelty, not only to animals but also to plants. Root vegetables (such as carrots) are forbidden because pulling them out of the ground means killing the plant.

Buddhism

The Buddha, who founded this faith, stated that all killing was wrong. However, meat is not forbidden, and many Buddhists today eat some meat.

Sikhism

Guru Nanak, the founder of Sikhism, said, "Only fools wrangle [argue] about meat." Sikhs are allowed to eat meat, except during religious ceremonies.

> *Halal butcher*

Some religions teach that meat must be prepared in a special way before it can be eaten. This is a Muslim halal butcher's shop.

Judaism

The Jewish religion allows its followers to eat all meat except for shellfish and meat from pigs. The meat must be butchered in the correct way, called "kosher" (meaning "fit" or "proper"). This means the butcher must kill the animal according to a special ritual. Then, the meat must be washed and soaked to remove all traces of blood.

Christianity

Christians have few rules concerning the eating of animals. In fact, the Bible encourages people to eat meat. In one early passage, God says, "Everything that lives and moves will be food for you."

Islam

Muslims can eat all sorts of meat, except for pork. All meat must be specially prepared so that it is "halal" (meaning "legal" or "allowed"). The correct Islamic texts must be recited when the animal is killed, and all blood must be drained or washed away. Islam also advises Muslims to eat only healthy foods.

> *Hunter and hunted*
A shot deer lies in the snow at the feet of its killer.

Killing For Food

If you want to eat an animal, someone has to kill it. Anyone who eats meat is part of the process that turns a living animal into a piece of dead meat. You have to come to terms with this fact.

Does that sound shocking? If you want to reach a balanced opinion about this subject, you have to be completely honest with yourself. You may have decided, after reading Chapter Three, that it is morally right to eat meat. Now, you have to make another decision. Can you face the physical reality of an animal's death?

Some people become vegetarians for moral reasons. They stop eating meat because they are deeply shocked by the idea of deliberately killing a fellow creature. Others are upset by the way meat animals are treated during their lives, or they believe that meat is an unhealthy food.

In order to produce enough meat for the huge number of human carnivores in the world, farmers have developed more efficient ways of raising animals. Thanks to what is called "factory farming," there is always plenty of cheap meat in the stores and supermarkets. However, these new methods often mean miserable lives for the animals themselves.

What's wrong with factory farming?

Here is a report that describes in great detail the inhumane treatment of chickens.

IT'S TIME FOR CHICKENS!

Chicken farming is outright cruel. Chicks are kept in sheds called broiler houses; "broiler" being an industry term for chickens killed for their flesh. Up to 100,000 birds are crammed in these houses, with less than half a square foot of space per bird (about the space of a computer screen). The floor is concrete and laid with sawdust, wood shavings or chopped straw; it soon becomes covered with the animals' excrement. The filth may attract rats and flies bringing disease.

Because the birds are forced to spend their entire lives standing in their own droppings, they are in terrible pain from burns to their feet and legs, breast blisters, and ulcerated feet. Many of the windowless sheds are artificially lit for 24 hours a day. This deters the chicks from sleeping and instead makes them eat more. A fat bird means more money.

Broiler chickens are ready for slaughter at 1.8kg/ 4 pounds live weight in six weeks—half the time it once took. They go to death with the bodies of adult chickens and the blue eyes and high-pitched "cheep" of little chicks.

The birds grow abnormally fast because they are fed high-protein feed, growth-promoting **antibiotics**, and are selectively bred to do so. The result is that the bones of many break under their ballooning weight and their hearts are frequently unable to cope. In fact, an article in the agricultural journal *Feedstuffs* stated, "According to experts broilers now grow so rapidly that the heart and lungs are not developed well enough to support the remainder of the body, resulting in congestive heart failure and tremendous death losses."

[Source: 2006 article from the website of Viva USA, a vegan organization that campaigns on behalf of animals killed for food and makes filmed investigations of factory farms]

> *Chicken factory*

These chickens are being raised for meat in the cramped conditions of a broiler shed.

Chickens are kept in these appalling conditions in most parts of the world. Millions of other farm animals are forced to live in cramped and unnatural places. Pigs are kept in metal crates and cattle are penned in bare "**feed lots**."

Now that you have read this story, ask yourself the same questions as before. Can you believe the facts in the report? Clearly, the reporter is trying to be as shocking as possible. Does this make his or her evidence less reliable?

There is another big question to ask, and it needs careful and critical thinking. The story is about the horrors of a modern chicken factory. But is it directly linked to the argument about eating animals? Is there a connection between this sort of cruelty and meat-eating? Or are they two separate issues? After all, many meat-eaters strongly disapprove of factory farming. They never eat broiler chicken or other meat raised in this way.

When does an animal turn into meat?

What is the real difference between animals and meat? A live pig in a field is an animal. A piece of dead pig is meat. Someone has killed it, cut it up, removed the skin and bone, cleaned it off, wrapped it in plastic, and put it on a supermarket shelf. It is the same material, but it has suddenly changed its name.

Why do we call them two different things? Is it because we want to forget where our food comes from? In a way, the live animal has disappeared, and we do not have to think about it. What we are planning to eat is no longer a piece of pig, but a piece of pork.

The real price of milk

Many people decide not to eat meat because they do not want to cause the death or mistreatment of animals. Most of these vegetarians are happy to eat cheese, butter, and other products made from milk. But do they know how dairy farming works?

For example, why do cows make milk? Like all other mammals, the mother cow produces milk in order to feed her calf immediately after it is born. Without a baby, she will have no milk. So, the dairy farmer has to make sure that his cows become pregnant about once a year.

When the calf is born, it starts to drink its mother's milk. But the farmer wants to sell the milk for human use. As soon as possible, he takes the calf away from its mother. He extracts the milk by machine and sends it to the dairy. The cow will continue giving milk for about nine months.

What happens to the calves? Some will be kept until they are old enough to be killed as **veal** (very young beef). Some female calves will be allowed to grow up and become mothers themselves. Most of the males, however, will be sent straight off to the slaughterhouse.

Do you think that there is a link between eating cheese and eating meat?

> *What are you really eating?*

The meat in this cheeseburger was once part of a living animal, although it now bears no resemblance to a cow.

 ## Slaughterhouse eyewitnesses

"Cattle dragged and choked . . . Knocking 'em four, five, ten times. Every now and then when they're stunned they come back to life, and they're up there agonizing. They're supposed to be re-stunned but sometimes they aren't and they'll go through the skinning process alive. If people were to see this, they'd probably feel really bad about it."
An inspector who worked for the USDA (U.S. Department of Agriculture) describes watching cattle being killed in a slaughterhouse in Texas

"If you visit the killing floor of a slaughterhouse, it will brand your soul for life."
Howard F. Lyman, Montana farmer and environmental campaigner

> *A balanced diet*

This meal has a healthy balance of food types,
including meat and fresh vegetables.

What Is Healthy Eating?

The first human meat-eaters were wanderers and hunters. Food was hard to find, and the flesh of animals gave them concentrated helpings of the fats, proteins, and other nutrients they needed to stay alive. Life was a struggle for survival. These early humans used a huge amount of energy in working, moving, and keeping warm. They got this from their food.

Should we still be eating the same sort of diet today? Very few of us have strenuous physical lives. In fact, a large number get little or no exercise at all. In a world of cars, central heating, and supermarkets, it is easy for most people to stay warm and well fed. We do not need the large helpings of proteins and fats that kept our early ancestors going.

Many scientists now believe that people in most developed countries are eating too much fat. This is causing many health problems, including heart disease and some types of cancer. Much of the fat is contained in the meat we eat. Should we stop eating animals for health reasons? On the other hand, do we know that a vegetarian diet will give us all the nutrients we need?

Is meat bad for your health?

Many people think that a vegetarian diet is better for us than a meat-eating diet. Meat contains a lot more fat, cholesterol, and other substances than vegetables do. Too much of these can lead to serious diseases in later life. However, other factors can have an effect here. Do vegetarians live healthier lives in general?

Here is some evidence, based on scientific studies. It examines some of the common diseases in developed countries. Look at it critically. Is it fact or opinion? Does it change your ideas about eating animals?

Cancer Studies in England and Germany show that vegetarians are about 40 percent less likely to develop cancer than meat-eaters.

Heart disease Vegetarian diets also help prevent heart disease. Animal products are the main source of saturated fat and the only source of cholesterol in the diet.

High blood pressure In the early 1900s, scientists found that people who ate no meat had lower blood pressure. They also discovered that vegetarian diets could, within two weeks, significantly reduce a person's blood pressure.

Diabetes Some types of **diabetes** can be better controlled and sometimes even eliminated through a low-fat, vegetarian diet, along with regular exercise.

Kidney stones Vegetarian diets have been shown to reduce the chances of forming **kidney stones**. The American Academy of Family Physicians notes that high animal protein intake is largely responsible for the high prevalence of kidney stones in the United States and other developed countries.

Gallstones High-cholesterol, high-fat diets (typical meat-based diets) are blamed for the formation of **gallstones**. The consumption of meaty diets, compared to vegetarian diets, has been shown to nearly double the risk of gallstones in women.

Osteoporosis Vegetarians are at a lower risk of **osteoporosis** (weakening of the bones). Meat forces **calcium** out of the body, so eating meat can promote bone loss. In nations with mainly vegetable diets, osteoporosis is less common than in the United States.

Asthma A 1985 Swedish study found that individuals with asthma practicing a vegan diet for a full year have less need for medications and fewer severe asthma attacks. Twenty-two of the 24 subjects reported improvement by the end of the year.

[Source: Physicians' Committee for Responsible Medicine, Washington, D.C.]

Critical thinking checklist

Remember to:

✔ Spot the difference between facts and opinions

✔ Assess the evidence fairly and completely

✔ Be aware that there are many different ways of looking at a topic

✔ Look out for bias: Where is the evidence coming from?

✔ Make use of different points of view to strengthen your own argument

✔ Support your own ideas with good reasons and strong, clear evidence

> *Good or bad?*
Many scientists believe modern fast food can make us fatter and less healthy.

Meat scares in the news

- Research Suggests Link Between Red Meat and Some Cancers
- Red Meat and Diabetes Linked
- Health Risks to Humans of Antibiotics in Meat and Poultry
- Rejecting Meat "keeps weight low"
- Non-Meat-Eaters Have Lower Rates of Hypertension and Lower Blood Pressures
- A Meat-Based Diet Is Dangerous for Your Heart's Health

These are some of the hundreds of headlines about the health dangers of meat-eating that appear in newspapers and on TV every year. There are very few stories that point out the benefits of eating meat. Why do you think this is?

Is meat good for your health?

Have you looked for evidence about meat and health? You may find that a lot of it is negative. There are plenty of vegetarian websites that point out the bad points about a meat-eating diet. Does meat have any good points?

The Bogalusa Heart Study, in Bogalusa, Louisiana, has been running for more than 30 years. The study has been finding out how heart disease develops in children and young adults. These are some of its findings:

Children who eat more meat are less likely to have deficiencies than those who eat little or no meat. Children who don't eat meat are more likely to feel tired, apathetic, unable to concentrate, are sick more often, more frequently depressed, and are the most likely to be **malnourished** and have stunted growth. Meat and other animal-source foods are the building blocks of healthy growth that have made America's youngsters among the tallest, strongest, and healthiest in the world.

Meat is an important source of quality nutrients. Even a small amount of meat can dramatically improve a poor diet. The nutrients in meat are highly concentrated, yet lean meat is relatively low in **calories**.

- *Proteins*   Proteins are important for children's healthy growth and development.

- *Iron*   The iron in meat is of high quality and well absorbed by the body, unlike iron from plants. More than 90 percent of iron may be wasted when taken without some iron from animal sources.

- *Zinc*   Meat, poultry, and eggs are also good sources of absorbable zinc, a trace **mineral** vital for strengthening the immune system and normal growth. Deficiencies link to decreased attention, poorer problem solving and short-term memory, weakened immune system, and the inability to fight infection.

- *Vitamin B12*   Found almost exclusively in animal products, Vitamin B12 is necessary for forming new cells. A deficiency can cause anemia and permanent nerve damage and paralysis.

[Source: Bogalusa Heart Study, Louisiana]

How healthy are vegetarians?

We have already seen plenty of evidence that shows the benefits of giving up meat-eating. But are there any risks in a vegetarian diet?

Some vegetarians consume a lot of food that contains just as much fat and cholesterol as meat does. Lacto-ovo vegetarians eat milk and eggs. These are high in animal fats, which can increase the danger of certain illnesses.

The Bogalusa study shows that a strict vegetarian diet may lack several important ingredients that help children to grow and develop normally. Eating disorder specialists and **pediatricians** are seeing alarming numbers of young children today with stunted growth, fragile bones, and stress fractures who have stopped eating meat and other animal-source foods.

> *The no-meat medalist*
> Vegetarian U.S. hurdler Ed Moses won Olympic medals and broke world records.

 What's in your burger?

Nutrition Facts: Burger King Triple Whopper Sandwich
Total weight: 16 oz. (456 g)

		% of daily needs
Calories:	1,130	52%
Total fat:	74 g (2.6 oz.)	114%
Carbohydrates:	51 g (1.8 oz.)	17%
Protein:	67 g (2.4 oz.)	135%
Sodium (salt):	1,160 mg (0.04 oz.)	48%
Cholesterol:	255 mg (0.009 oz.)	85%

> *Monster crops*

Gigantic fields of grain need enormous gas-guzzling machines to harvest them.

Meat And The Environment

Which industry is the biggest in the world? The answer is farming. It is easily the biggest, and it has been for thousands of years. Today, farms of all kinds cover more than 37 percent of the world's land area. As the world's population grows, it needs more food to eat, so more land has to be plowed to grow crops or graze livestock. At present, the area of farmland is growing by nearly 1 percent every year.

Just over half of this land is used to raise farm animals. This means that a huge proportion of Earth's surface (about 19 percent) is devoted to producing meat and dairy food. The animals do not just eat grass. They also consume a large amount of the world's food crops. Is this a waste of resources? Should we be growing more food plants instead?

But vegetable crops also use up a lot of precious resources. Woodland has to be cleared of trees so that crops can be sown. Once it is cleared, **arable land** needs regular doses of fertilizer and other chemicals to help the plants grow. Plows, sprayers, harvesters, and other pieces of machinery pollute the air with their carbon emissions. Is this any better?

Does livestock farming harm the environment?

Meat Is a Global Warming Issue

The production of meat significantly increases global warming. Cow farms produce millions of tons of carbon dioxide (CO_2) and **methane** per year, the two major **greenhouse gases** that together account for more than 90 percent of U.S. greenhouse emissions.

The 2004 *State of the World* spells out the link between animals raised for meat and global warming: "Livestock emit 16 percent of the world's annual production of methane, a powerful greenhouse gas."

Additionally, rain forests are being cut down at an extremely rapid rate to both pasture cows and grow soybeans to feed cows. This not only creates more greenhouse gases through the process of destruction, but also reduces the amazing benefits that those trees provide. Rain forests have been called the "lungs of the Earth," because they filter our air by absorbing CO_2, while emitting life-supporting oxygen.

[Source: Dan Brook, "E," the *Environmental Magazine*, July 2006]

What are the two main environmental dangers posed by animal farming, according to this article? First, cattle produce an enormous amount of harmful gases that make global warming worse. Second, farmers are cutting down large areas of rain forest to make way for grazing animals.

Clearly, livestock farming is causing a lot of damage to our environment. The damage is only likely to increase. The world population is already about 6.5 billion, and in 20 years it will probably reach 8 billion. All these extra people will need food. Do you think we should continue to raise more animals to eat? Or should we stop eating meat altogether?

Pollution and disease

Do our meat-eating habits create any other dangers for the planet? Pollution from farming is a rapidly growing problem. The most obvious polluters are the animals themselves. Can you imagine how much waste matter (dung and urine) is produced by more than 50 billion cows, sheep, pigs, and poultry in one year? This can easily leak into rivers and springs, making the water unfit to drink.

> *Trees or meat?*

Cattle graze on farmland in Madagascar, in Africa, that was created by cutting down rain forest.

Modern farming methods have also led to the spread of deadly diseases. The most famous of these is BSE (Bovine Spongiform Encephalopathy), better known as Mad Cow Disease. This was possibly caused when brain and nerve material from dead sheep was mixed into cattle food. Since 1984 many thousands of cattle have died from BSE, and a related infection has killed at least 150 humans worldwide.

"The human appetite for animal flesh is a driving force behind virtually every major category of environmental damage now threatening the human future—deforestation, erosion, fresh water scarcity, pollution, climate change, and the spread of disease."
World Watch, 2004

 How many animals do we eat?

The average U.S. resident lives for 75 years. During that time, he or she will eat the equivalent of:

✔ 11 cows

✔ 32 pigs and sheep

✔ 2,600 chickens, turkeys, and other birds

Number of land animals killed for food during 2005 in the United States: 10,450,000,000

What does it take to raise animals?

What is the job of a pig or a beef cow? It is quite simple: to convert the energy of plants into food for humans. The animal eats vegetable matter and turns it into meat. Unfortunately, animals are not very efficient converters of energy. A chicken, for example, produces only one unit of energy for every three units it eats. That is a ratio of 3:1. Cattle are even worse. Their ratio is an amazing 16:1.

What sort of food do farm animals need? To grow quickly, most of them have to be fed on much more than grass. Special animal feeds are made from corn and other grains, beans, and many other ingredients. All of these have to be grown as crops in the first place, taking up more valuable farmland.

On the other hand, cattle and some other animals can be fed on by-products, such as the rinds of sugarcane and shells of cotton seed, which would otherwise go to waste. Sheep and other grazing (grass-eating) animals can also survive on difficult or poor quality land that cannot be plowed.

What does it take to grow crops?

Would it be better for the world's environment if we grew more crops and fewer animals? Are rice and soybeans less harmful to Earth than pigs and cattle? Certainly, plants are much more efficient than animals in converting energy into human food. But what are their disadvantages?

In many ways, growing grain and vegetables is not very different from raising livestock. Land has to be cleared of trees and other unwanted plants. Modern farmers use a huge array of powerful chemicals to help the crops grow as fast as possible. There are sprays to kill weeds, insect pests, and disease spores, and there are also many kinds of fertilizer. Rain washes these chemicals off the soil and into lakes and rivers, where they can cause a lot of damage.

> *Arable Amazon*

These bags contain soybeans grown on land that was once untouched Amazon rain forest.

> *Thirsty plants*
Grain and other vegetable crops need a huge
amount of water to grow successfully.

 ## Crops vs. animals and land use

Amount of energy produced in different ways on 2.5 acres (1 hectare) of land (in millions of kilocalories)			
Grain	5	Beef	0.4
Rice	7	Eggs	0.5
Potatoes	12	Milk	1.8
Cassava	12		
Banana	13		
Sugar	25		
Area of land needed to produce a year's supply of protein for one adult in acres (hectares)			
Beans	0.6 (0.25)	Dairy cows	2.5–7.4 (1–3)
Grass	0.7–1.5 (0.3–0.6)	Chickens	7.4 (3)
Cereals	1.5 (0.6)	Sheep	4.9–12.4 (2–5)
Potatoes	1.7 (0.7)	Pigs	12.4 (5)
		Beef	7.4–14.8 (3–6)

> *Eating out*

Can we change our eating habits so that we cause
less damage to the environment?

Can We Change Things?

By now, you should have a better idea of what you think about using animals as food. You may have decided it is wrong to eat meat, and that vegetarian living is the only moral and practical way forward for humans. Or you may believe that meat is a natural part of our diet, and it is right to kill animals to eat them.

Whatever you think, one thing is clear. The modern farming industry often treats animals in a cruel and unhealthy way. Many creatures live and die in terrible conditions. The result is not just misery for them, but also the increasing chance that the meat we eat may be polluted with chemicals or disease. Moreover, the growing demand for meat is causing harm to the environment.

Can we do anything to change this? Can we continue to eat animals if so many of them are raised in this horrible way? A growing number of livestock farmers throughout the world are introducing more caring and humane methods. These include using only feeds and fertilizers that are organically produced. But does this mean that less meat will be available? Will it become more expensive?

Can farming methods be improved?

Modern factory farming shocks many people. They see cattle, pigs, and poultry being raised and slaughtered in appalling conditions. But is it right to blame the farmers for this? After all, they are simply trying to produce a supply of meat that is cheap and plentiful. The worldwide demand for meat is growing steadily.

Is there an alternative? Are there farming methods that treat animals kindly, while at the same time protecting the environment from chemical pollution? Several charities and agricultural bodies are campaigning for more humane systems of livestock farming. Some farmers are going back to traditional ways of looking after their animals, such as allowing chickens to grow "free range" outdoors. Others are using only natural fertilizers and animal feeds.

```
The five freedoms for farm animals:
● Freedom from thirst, hunger, and malnutrition (Access
  to fresh water and a proper diet)
● Freedom from discomfort
  (A suitable environment, including shelter and resting
  area)
● Freedom from pain, injury, and disease
  (Proper medical care)
● Freedom to express normal behavior
  (Space to roam in, the company of
  fellow animals)
● Freedom from fear and distress
  (No mental suffering)

[Source: GAP, the Good Agricultural Practice plan,
pioneered by the Compassion in World Farming Trust]
```

Can we change the way we eat?

Apart from the farmers, who else is to blame for the horrors of factory farming? Anybody who eats meat has a part in the way that meat is produced. If we want cheap burgers and fried chicken, we have to accept that the mass-production methods will stay. There is a direct link between the broiler chicken shed and the fast-food restaurant.

Is there an alternative? Obviously, there is one sure way to get rid of factory farms. We have to realize that we should pay more money for our meat and get used to eating less of it. This will mean that farmers do not have to raise so many animals, while earning the same amount for selling their meat. The result of this will be that they can look after their livestock better.

> *Snouts in the trough*
These large white sows are being fed in cages on an intensive pig farm.

 # Running out of room

All humans need a certain amount of space to supply their needs for water, air, and growing food. Scientists calculate that humans need at least 2.5 acres (1 hectare) of room each. But this figure does not include space for all the domestic animals we raise. The number of humans and meat animals is growing very quickly, and Earth is getting dangerously overcrowded.

How much room do humans have on Earth in 2007?
4.9 acres (2 hectares) each

Add farm animals, and how much room do we all have?
0.7 acres (0.3 hectares) each

How much room will humans have in 2050?
3.7 acres (1.5 hectares) each

Add farm animals, and how much room will we all have in 2050?
0.5 acres (0.2 hectares) each

What is the point of food?

Why do we eat food at all? One answer is obvious: to stay alive. Food is the fuel that keeps our bodies moving and working. The better the quality of the food, the better our bodies work.

But is there another answer? Preparing and eating good food is one of the pleasures of life. We can get great enjoyment from the taste, texture, appearance, and smell of a well-cooked dish. Fine food is also at the center of most of our celebrations, from birthday parties to seasonal festivals. Sitting down to a meal with our family or friends is often an important part of our social life.

How do you view eating? Do you regularly eat around a table with other people? Many people today treat food as nothing more than fuel, like putting gasoline in a car. They do not care where the fuel comes from or how it was produced, as long as it fills them up.

Respect what you eat

Does this matter? It certainly matters if you are part of the process of killing and eating animals. If you do not care where your meat was grown or how it was butchered, then you can hardly care about animals being treated cruelly. If you are a vegetarian, this does not matter so much. Plants do not suffer pain or distress (as far as we know), so they cannot be treated cruelly.

The important thing is to respect your food. If you eat meat, you should care about the animal it came from. Traditional hunting peoples, such as the San Bushmen of Africa, have a close understanding of the animals they chase and kill. Surely we should do the same?

> *Living off the land*

A San hunter of the Kalahari Desert in Africa comes home with a deer he has caught in a trap.

> *Death trip*
Pigs are loaded into a truck to be driven to the slaughterhouse.

 What do they think?

"I grew up a hunter. All our boys and men were hunters. Hunting is going and talking to the animals. You don't steal. You go and ask. You set a trap or go with bow or spear. It can take days. You track the antelope. He knows you are there, he knows he has to give you his strength. But he runs and you have to run. As you run, you become like him. It can last hours and exhaust you both. You talk to him and look into his eyes. And then he knows he must give you his strength so your children can live."

Roy Sesana, a San Bushman of the Kalahari

"In the fast-food culture food is not given but taken, which is one reason why, in such a culture, nobody is properly 'at home.' The solitary stuffing of burgers, pizzas, and TV dinners; the disappearance of family meals and domestic cooking; the loss of table manners—all these tend to obscure the distinction between eating and feeding."

Roger Scruton, "Eating Our Friends" (article in Right Reason *magazine, May 2006)*

How to organize your own debate

Should we eat animals? Have you formed your own opinion yet? If you have, the next stage is to explain your opinion to other people and persuade them that you are right. The best way to do this is to organize a debate with your classmates.

The word "organize" is an important one. If 20 students get together and start arguing, you are likely to end up with a shouting match. You will not learn anything from that. Your debate has to have rules and a structure that everybody agrees to.

What kind of debate?

There are many debate formats to choose from. The simplest of all is a classroom debate, in which every student gets a chance to argue his or her opinion. In a formal debate, you start with a motion (a question or a statement) to argue about. For instance, is it wrong to eat animals? A panel of speakers (usually two teams of two) represents each side of the argument. They each make short speeches, arguing their case. Then, they answer questions from the rest of the students. Lastly, the audience members may vote to show whether or not they agree with the motion. The essential ingredient for a debate is opposing viewpoints. One side argues in favor of a topic. This is called the proposition. The other side argues against the case made by the first speaker. This is called the opposition. Set a time limit for the whole debate. If possible, keep the total running time to under 90 minutes. You should also set time limits of no longer than five minutes for each of the opening speeches. Choose someone to be the **moderator** (referee). This person does not take part in the debate but rather directs it, introducing the topic and keeping control of the speakers. Nobody may speak unless the moderator permits. A good moderator should treat both sides equally.

> *School debate*

A student argues her case.

> *Room to roam*
Beef cattle graze in wide-open spaces.

What happens?

The moderator explains the motion and the topic for debate. Then, the four speakers on the panel take turns reading their prepared speeches. One argues the case for the motion and the second speaks against it. The third speaks for it and the fourth against. After this, the moderator will ask the audience to pose questions to the speakers. The debate ends with a short closing statement from each side, when they restate their opinions with strong supporting evidence. Then, the audience votes, either for or against the motion.

 How to be a good debater

✔ Research your subject well in advance
✔ Have plenty of facts and evidence ready
✔ Speak only when the moderator allows you to
✔ Listen carefully to what other people say
✔ Allow other people to express their opinions and do not interrupt
✔ Speak clearly and loudly enough for the audience to hear
✔ Focus on the most important points in your argument
✔ Note the weak points in your opponent's speech

What do you think now?

Did you have a definite opinion about eating animals when you started reading this book? Or had you never really thought about the subject before? The book is not aimed at convincing you one way or another. Its purpose is to show you both sides of the debate and give you tips on how to think, how to look at evidence, and how to argue your case.

Here is a quick survey of the main arguments for and against eating animals that we have looked at in this book.

Carnivore or vegetarian?

Is the human body adapted to eat meat? We started out as plant-eaters, but later began eating animals. These were a better source of protein and other nutrients and probably helped humans to develop larger brains than most other mammals.

Right or wrong?

There is a fundamental moral question about whether we have the right to kill animals. Do animals feel pain, distress, happiness, and other emotions in the same way we do? Should we be ending the lives of other creatures just so that we can feed ourselves? We actually kill countless animals every day, either by accident or because we think of them as pests.

Cruel or kind?

Modern livestock farming, with its battery cages and huge slaughterhouses, often treats animals in a barbaric way. How can we continue to eat meat when we know how horribly it may have been produced? But many meat-eaters condemn factory farming just as fiercely as vegetarians do. Moreover, the production of milk often involves a lot of cruelty.

Healthy or unhealthy?

Is meat bad for us? Figures show that meat-eaters are more likely to suffer from heart disease and other dangerous illnesses. This is due to the high levels of some fats and other substances in animal flesh. But people who eat no meat at all can miss out on important nutrients in their food, such as crucial vitamins and minerals.

Animals or plants?

Environmental issues have never been more urgent. How much harm to the planet is caused by livestock farming? The growing demand for meat means that more room has to be found for meat animals. Meat production also causes major pollution problems in many parts of the world. But is plant growing, with its herbicides and fertilizers, any less harmful?

> *Making your point*

A demonstrator dressed as a chicken protests against cruelty to animals outside a school in Louisiana.

Find Out More

Projects

- Check out your belongings. How many items contain some kind of animal product? Look especially for leather (shoes, straps, gloves) or horn (buttons).
- What is in your food? Read the labels of jars and packaging, especially the "ingredients" section. Look up anything you do not recognize. If there is meat in it, how is the meat described?
- If you are a meat-eater, find out where your meat comes from. Ask in stores. Try to discover where you can buy meat produced as locally as possible.
- Look up "**organic farms**" and see if there is one near you that allows visitors. Both vegetarians and meat-eaters can learn a lot by seeing livestock being raised humanely and healthily.

Books

- Burnie, David. *Endangered Planet*. Boston: Kingfisher, 2004.
  A study of the effect we are having on Earth.
- Kallen, Stuart A. (ed.). *Is Factory Farming Harming America?* Farmington Hills, Mich.: Greenhaven, 2006.
- Schlosser, Eric, and Charles Wilson. *Chew on This: Everything You Don't Want to Know About Fast Food.* Boston: Houghton Mifflin, 2006.
  This book tells the shocking truth about burgers and fries.
- Winkler, Kathleen. *Vegetarianism and Teens: A Hot Issue*. Berkeley Heights, N.J.: Enslow, 2001.

Websites

Food and environmental agencies

www.fao.org
The Food and Agriculture Organization, part of the
World Health Organization

www.usda.gov
The U.S. Department of Agriculture

www.epa.gov
The U.S. Environmental Protection Agency

Attacking the meat industry

www.meat.org
Be warned: this site has some disturbing images

www.themeatrix.com
Includes animation about the horrors of factory farming

Vegetarianism

Simply type "vegetarian" into a search engine and you will get plenty of sites

Glossary

antibiotics   medicines containing substances, such as penicillin, which destroy organisms causing disease

arable land   farmland that is plowed for growing crops

biased   in favor of one particular view or argument; not open-minded

broiler chicken   chicken killed at a young age for grilling or roasting

calcium   element that is an important part of our bones and teeth

calorie   unit used to measure heat; it can be used to show the amounts of energy contained in different foods

canine teeth   dog-like teeth; used to describe the four pointed front teeth of humans

carbohydrate   sugary and starchy chemical compound found in food

catalyst   something or someone that sets off a big event

cholesterol   white substance found in foods that can cause various diseases

diabetes   disease that prevents the body from processing sugars in the blood and urine properly, leading to weakness and sometimes death

feed lot   enclosed area where animals such as cattle are fattened as fast as possible before slaughter

fundamental   basic or central

gallstone   small, hard object in the digestive system made of cholesterol or calcium

greenhouse gas   gas (especially carbon dioxide) that helps to absorb the heat of the sun, thus making the atmosphere warmer

kidney stone   small, hard object formed in the kidney

malnourished   suffering from poor quality food or too little food

methane   colorless gas made mostly from carbon (a major greenhouse gas)

mineral   naturally occurring substance, such as zinc or iron. Some minerals are essential to animal health.

moderator   person who leads a meeting or assembly

nutrient   something in food that nourishes or feeds us healthily

organic farming   method of growing crops and raising livestock using only fertilizers and other chemicals made from plants or animals

osteoporosis   disease in which the bones become brittle and easily fractured

pediatrician   doctor who deals with the care of babies and young children

primitive   belonging to the earliest or original stage of something

protein   chemical compound that plays an important part in health, especially the growth and repair of body cells

ratio   relation between two things expressed in numbers

slaughterhouse   factory where meat animals are killed and butchered

veal   meat that comes from a calf

vegan   person who eats no meat, eggs, or dairy products

vitamin   substances found naturally in plants and some animals that are essential for good health

Index